THE
FESTIVE FOOD
OF
ITALY

Maddalena Bonino

ILLUSTRATED BY SALLY MALTBY

SERIES EDITOR: HENRIETTA GREEN

A Bulfinch Press Book
Little, Brown and Company
Boston • Toronto • London

First North American Edition

First published 1991 by
Kyle Cathie Limited
3 Vincent Square London SW1P 2LX
ISBN 0-8212-1885-9

Library of Congress Catalog Card Number

Library of Congress Cataloging-in-Publication
information is available.

Bulfinch Press is an imprint and trademark of
Little, Brown and Company (Inc.)
Published simultaneously in Canada by Little,
Brown & Company (Canada) Limited

Designed by Geoff Hayes

PRINTED IN BELGIUM

Contents

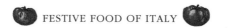

San Silvestro

NEW YEAR'S EVE

Saint Silvester, to whom the last day of the year is dedicated, was Pope in the fourth century during the reign of Constantine, and contributed to making Christianity a recognized faith legalized by the emperor. New Year's Eve is a festival when secular and religious rites combine. Janus, the two-faced god, gives his name to the first month of the year as he can look both backwards and forwards, and this is the time when people sum up the results of the past year and look to the future. On the stroke of midnight windows are opened and fireworks light up the sky. The floor is swept of old dust, and in the south the more drastic measure is taken to break with the past of throwing out of the window broken crockery, pots and pans, and sometimes even furniture.

Grand dinners are organized; traditionally fish will appear as one of the courses, and stuffed pig's trotter served with lentils, which symbolize coins and are said to bring wealth if eaten on this day.

Gnocchi di Patate al Sugo

(POTATO DUMPLINGS WITH TOMATO SAUCE)
serves 4
1kg/2¼lb floury potatoes
225g/8oz/2cups plain flour, plus flour for dusting
1 pinch of salt
1 quantity tomato sauce (below)
100g/3½oz/1cup grated Parmesan

1 Boil the potatoes in salted water until tender. Peel and mash while still hot, turn onto a floured surface, sprinkle with half the flour and season with the salt. Mix to a soft, slightly sticky dough, incorporating the rest of the flour.

2 Shape the dough into rolls the thickness of a thumb and cut into 2cm/¾in pieces. Roll each piece on the prongs of a fork or the side of a grater to mark them (this will ensure faster and more thorough cooking).

3 Drop each *gnocco* on a floured teatowel, making sure the *gnocchi* do not touch each other or they will stick.

4 Cook a few *gnocchi* at a time in boiling water, for 5–8 minutes. Remove with a slotted spoon to a warm serving dish and ladle a little warmed sauce over each layer.

5 When all the *gnocchi* are cooked, finish with the remaining sauce and sprinkle with the Parmesan.

Tomato sauce
1 small carrot, finely chopped
1 small onion, finely chopped
1 stalk of celery, finely chopped
40ml/2tablespoons/3tablespoons
  olive oil
400g/14oz can of plum tomatoes,
  chopped
2 bay leaves
5ml/1teaspoon sugar
115g/4oz/½cup butter, cut into
  cubes
salt and freshly ground pepper

1 Fry the carrot, onion and celery in the oil until just coloured, add the tomatoes, bay leaves, seasoning and sugar.

2 Simmer until the vegetables are tender and either pass through a sieve and then incorporate the butter for a smooth sauce or add the butter and leave chunky.

Pesce Arrosto
(ROAST FISH)

Any type of fish on the bone can be used for this recipe: brill, turbot, monkfish, sea bass, etc.

serves 4

2 mullets, together weighing about 1kg/2¼lb
   scaled and gutted
75ml/5tablespoons/⅓cup olive oil
50ml/3tablespoons/¼cup balsamic vinegar or white
   wine vinegar
115g/4oz each of stoned green olives and capers
small bunch of flat-leaf parsley, finely chopped
salt and freshly ground pepper

1 Sprinkle 40ml/2tablespoons/3tablespoons of the olive oil into a roasting tray, arrange the fish in it, sprinkle with remaining oil, half the vinegar, all the olives and capers, and season.
2 Bake in a preheated 200°C/400°F/gas6 oven for about 30 minutes, depending on fish thickness.
3 Place the fish on a serving dish and keep warm. Reduce the cooking juices for a few seconds, add the remaining vinegar and the parsley and pour over the fish.

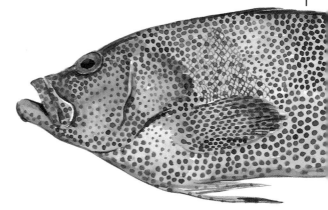

Torrone di Sesamo

(SESAME NOUGAT)

250g/8½oz/1½cups sesame seeds
200g/7oz/1½cups honey
50g/2oz/¼cup sugar
75g/2½oz/½cup whole almonds, roasted and
  chopped
40ml/2tablespoons/3tablespoons almond oil or
  sunflower oil

1 Melt the honey over low heat, add the sugar and
bring to the boil, stirring constantly.
2 Add the sesame seeds and, still stirring, boil for
a further 5 minutes. Add the almonds and keep
cooking for 5–10 minutes until the mixture feels
denser.
3 Pour the mixture preferably onto an oiled
marble surface, or any cold surface, and flatten
with an oiled rolling pin while still hot.
4 Leave to cool a little then with a sharp knife
score into squares or diamonds and leave to cool.
Stored in an airtight tin in a cool dry place, the
nougat will last for a few months.

Sagra del Mandorlo in Fiore

FEAST OF THE FLOWERING ALMOND TREE

While the rest of Italy is still in the grip of winter, Sicily is celebrating the thaw and the coming of spring, heralded by the blossoming of the almond trees. During the first ten days of February a festival is held at Agrigento, a beautiful piece of countryside scattered with Greek ruins, almond trees and orange groves, in conjunction with a festival of folklore; while traditional dancers and singers show off their talents in the open air using the Greek amphitheatre as a stage, visitors sample the region's delicacies and enjoy the spectacle, surrounded by the scent of flowering almond trees.

The eighteen varieties of almond grown in Sicily are a fundamental ingredient in the local cuisine and in the preparation of celebratory dishes, which still reflect a strong Arab influence, especially in the use of honey, nuts and spices, and in the elaborate preparation involved. The time-consuming job of preparing some of these feast sweets fell at one time to the nuns, who it was thought would have sufficient time to make them. 'Martorana Fruit' is one example, taking its name from a convent near Palermo, where the nuns still prepare marzipan, shape it and paint it to resemble all sorts of fruit and vegetables. During the fourteenth century this activity was temporarily halted in some convents by the religious authorities, as the nuns were neglecting their spiritual duties in favour of constructing these delicious sweets.

Fiore di Mandorlo
(ALMOND BISCUITS)

These 'Flowers of Mandorlo' are so called because of the shape they take on while cooking.

Makes about 30 biscuits
450g/1lb/4cups ground almonds
225g/8oz/1cup sugar
125g/4½oz/⅓cup honey
5ml/1teaspoon ground cinnamon
grated zest of 1 lemon
1 or 2 egg whites
icing sugar to sprinkle

1 Mix together the ground almonds, sugar, honey, cinnamon and lemon zest with enough egg white to make a firm paste. Knead until smooth.

2 Shape into rounds and bake on a greased tray in a preheated 150°C/300°F/gas2 oven for about 20 minutes.

3 Leave to cool, then sprinkle with icing sugar.

Carnevale

The days before Ash Wednesday are eagerly awaited throughout Italy, as every village and town prepares to celebrate the annual *Carnevale*. Each carnival has a distinct character, celebrating a town or village's own historical connections, and some of the larger ones are well known, attracting visitors from all over the world. The oldest and best known is probably that of Venice, during which the whole city comes alive with masked and costumed revellers parading and processing through Venice's maze of streets.

A very different carnival takes place in Viareggio, in Tuscany, where gigantic floats and papier-mâché caricatures of public figures form a spectacular procession through the town's streets. In Ivrea, in Piedmont, the festivities commemorate the town's insurrection and end of feudal tyranny; after four days of costumed pageants and processions the insurrection is re-enacted, using oranges as ammunition. All ends well in the town square, where everyone meets to enjoy a rich and filling bean stew, 'La Fagiolata', the last over-indulgence before the restrictions of Lent.

Fagiolata
(BEAN STEW)

serves 6

550g/1¼lb dried borlotti beans soaked overnight
450g/1lb belly of pork, cut into cubes
1 large onion, diced
50g/2oz/½cup butter
40ml/2tablespoons/3tablespoons olive oil
450g/1lb ripe tomatoes (plum tomatoes if possible), roughly chopped
2 bay leaves
sprig of thyme
salt and freshly ground pepper

1 Put soaked beans, pork belly and onion in a pot, cover with water and bring to the boil. Simmer until beans are soft.

2 In a frying-pan heat the butter and oil; when sizzling add the tomatoes, bay leaves and thyme, and cook for a few minutes.

3 Drain the beans and return to the pot with the tomato mixture. Simmer for another 30 minutes and adjust seasoning. Serve hot with bread or polenta.

Italian sausages (*cotechini*) can be added to this rich stew; boil these separately, slice and add in the last 10 minutes of cooking.

Chiacchiere

(GOSSIPS)

These traditional carnival sweets vary from region to region, and are known variously as *cenci* (rags), *nodi* (knots), *sfrappole* (bits and pieces), and so on. Grappa is sometimes used instead of Marsala, and lemon rind, cinnamon and aniseed can be added for a different flavour. They are all delicious, especially when served with a glass of sweet or sparkling wine.

450g/1lb/4cups plain flour, and extra for dusting
100g/3½oz/½cup sugar
50g/2oz/¼cup butter, softened
3 eggs
50ml/3tablespoons/¼cup Marsala
5ml/1teaspoon vanilla essence
oil for deep-frying
icing sugar for sprinkling

1 Sift the flour into a bowl, make a well in the centre and add the sugar, butter, eggs, Marsala and vanilla. Mix well to form a dough. Turn out and knead on a floured surface until smooth.
2 Roll out thinly with a rolling pin or pass through a pasta machine until the dough is as thin as a sheet of lasagne. Cut the dough into strips.
3 Heat the oil in a deep-frying pan, and when very hot fry a few strips at a time until golden. Remove with a slotted spoon and drain on kitchen paper. Sprinkle with icing sugar.

Pasqua

EASTER

Easter is the most important feast in the religious calendar and is celebrated widely as a religious and secular festival. The word *Pasqua* derives from the Jewish Pasch-Passover, and indeed Easter is a time of transition from winter to spring, from the preparations and restrictions of Lent into the rejoicing and celebration of the Resurrection. Lamb, eggs and wheat always feature in Easter meals, lamb representing Christ, and also symbolizing spring, the egg being the secular symbol of life and wheat the symbol of resurrection. In some parts of Italy it is still customary for farmers to take lambs and wheat to church on Good Friday to be blessed.

During the last week of Lent all sorts of special sweets and cakes are eaten; every region has its own speciality, but marzipan or chocolate reclining lambs bearing Christ's flag of victory can be found in all pâtisseries, as are *colombe*, dove-shaped cakes similar to *panettone*, *Pastiera Napoletana*, a delicious cake which includes cooked wheat, fresh Ricotta and orange candied peel, and of course chocolate eggs.

Easter Monday *(Pasquetta)* is traditionally spent picnicking in the warm spring air, with family and friends; in town or in country, good company and

plenty of wine are all that are needed, and of course good simple Italian picnic food: vegetable, meat and pasta pies, cheeses, hams and sausages, breads, pizzas and *focaccias*.

Agnello Brodettato
(LAMB WITH EGG AND LEMON SAUCE)
serves 6

1kg/2¼lb shoulder or leg of lamb, cut into cubes
50ml/3tablespoons/¼cup olive oil
1 large onion, finely sliced
85g/3oz Parma ham, diced
2.5ml/½teaspoon grated nutmeg
4tablespoons plain flour
250ml/⅓pint/1cup lamb stock
150ml/¼pint/⅔cup dry white wine
3 egg yolks
juice of 1 lemon
small bunch of parsley, finely chopped
freshly ground pepper

1 Heat the oil in a saucepan and add the sliced onion and cubed ham. Season with plenty of pepper and the nutmeg.
2 Toss the cubed lamb in the flour, add to the onion and ham and fry gently until all pieces are golden.
3 Pour in the stock and simmer until almost evaporated, then add white wine, season with a little more pepper, cover and leave to simmer for about 2 hours.
4 Lift the lamb pieces out of the saucepan, place in a serving dish and keep warm.
5 Whisk the egg yolks and lemon juice and stir into the cooking juices away from the heat. Pour over the lamb, sprinkle with chopped parsley, and serve immediately.

Torta Pasqualina
(EASTER PIE)

Traditionally there are thirty-three pastry layers in this Ligurian pie, one for each year of Christ's life; each layer is brushed with a feather dipped in oil, and then air is blown between the layers with a straw to help the pastry rise.

serves 6–8
1kg/2¼lb beet leaves or spinach
115g/4oz/1cup fresh breadcrumbs
250ml/⅓pint/1cup milk
10 eggs
200g/7oz/2cups grated Parmesan
550g/1¼lb fresh Ricotta
3 sprigs of fresh marjoram
225g/8oz/1cup butter
20 sheets filo pastry

1 To make the filling, quickly blanch the beets, drain well and squeeze out all excess water, then chop finely. Mix together the breadcrumbs and the milk and then stir in four of the eggs, half the grated Parmesan, the Ricotta, the chopped beets and marjoram leaves. Season and set aside.
2 Melt two-thirds of the butter. Lightly grease a 24cm /9in loose-bottomed cake tin. Line with a sheet of filo and brush with melted butter; lay over this nine further sheets, brushing each one with melted butter and taking care to cover the tin's sides.
3 Fill the cake tin with the beet mixture. Make six pockets in the mixture and into each put a dot of butter and break an egg, then sprinkle with the remaining Parmesan and season.
4 Cover with the remaining ten sheets of filo, brushing each layer with butter. Trim off excess.
5 Bake in a preheated 180°C/350°F/gas4 oven for about 45 minutes, and serve warm or cold.

Sagra del Carciofo
FESTIVAL OF THE ARTICHOKE

The artichoke is native to Italy, becoming popular around the time of the Renaissance, when it made frequent appearances at the banqueting tables of the time as both an ingredient and as a decorative centrepiece. Nowadays artichokes are grown and eaten in great quantity, cooked or eaten raw tossed in Parmesan and good olive oil.

During April and May dozens of villages across Italy celebrate the harvest of the artichoke, when the crops are taken in large crates and boxes to the market square where they are praised for size and quality; some find their way into large frying-pans to be offered with other local favourite specialities, where for the over-indulgent a glass of Cynar, a digestive made from the juice of artichokes, might be the order of the day.

Carciofi Fritti
(FRIED ARTICHOKES)

serves 4
8 small artichoke hearts, trimmed and quartered
  (keep in water and lemon juice)
350g/12oz/3cups plain flour
2 eggs, beaten
olive oil for frying
2 lemons
salt and freshly ground pepper

1 Drain and pat dry the artichoke segments. Toss in seasoned flour, then dip in the beaten eggs.
2 Heat olive oil in a frying-pan and fry a few pieces of artichoke at a time, turning occasionally, until golden. Drain on kitchen paper and serve hot with lemon wedges.

Carciofi alia Romana
(ARTICHOKES ROMAN STYLE)

serves 4

8 small or 4 large artichokes
bunch of flat-leafed parsley, finely chopped
1 garlic clove, finely chopped
8 sprigs of fresh mint, finely chopped
50ml/3tablespoons/¼cup olive oil
salt and freshly ground pepper

1 Remove the tough outer leaves of the artichokes and trim stalks. Loosen the inner leaves and with a sharp knife remove the choke. Place the prepared artichokes in a bowl of water and lemon juice to prevent discoloration.
2 Mix together the parsley, garlic and mint with enough olive oil to make the mixture wet, then season.
3 Stuff the artichokes with the herb mixture and re-close leaves as tightly as possible.
4 Fit the artichokes upside-down in a deep earthenware dish so that there is no space between them. Season well, then fill the dish with one part water and two parts oil, cover dish with lid or silver foil and bake in a preheated 160°C/325°F/gas3 oven for about 1 hour.
5 Drain and serve hot or cold.

Sagra delle Ciliege

THE CHERRY FESTIVAL

Fruit is usually served at the end of most Italian meals, and June marks the appearance on the table of bowls of luscious scarlet cherries.

Many varieties of cherry are grown all over Italy; Vignola in Emilia-Romagna is said to supply most of the cherries eaten in Europe, and its high concentration of trees makes it a very attractive place to visit in spring when the trees are in full bloom and in summer when they are laden with deep red fruit. Maraschino and Amarene cherries, which grow in the south, and the large, dark and sweet Visciole, from which Visner, a special sun-fermented liqueur, is made, are just some of the very popular varieties.

Cherry festivals are particularly joyous affairs; cartloads and basketfuls of cherries are taken to the market square and people come from the surrounding villages to buy crates to make enough jams, pickles and preserves to last the winter and to make traditional sweets and cakes such as *Dolce Amore* (a cake layered with cherry jam, sponge fingers, liqueurs and *zabajon*), and *Tortelli di Carnevale* (Carnival pastries).

Crostata di Ciliege
(CHERRY TART)

serves 6–8
Pastry
175g/6½oz/1½cups plain flour
45g/1½oz/⅙cup sugar
125g/4½oz/½cup chilled butter, cut into cubes
1 egg yolk
1 teaspoon vanilla essence

Filling
175g/6½oz fresh or bottled cherries
1 egg + 1 egg yolk
25g/1oz/⅛cup sugar
finely grated zest of 1 lemon
25g/1oz/¼cup plain flour
250ml/⅓pint/1cup double cream

1 First make the pastry. Combine the flour, sugar
and butter in a food processor until the mixture
resembles breadcrumbs, or rub together with your
fingers. Then quickly mix in the egg yolk and
vanilla essence. Turn onto a lightly floured surface
and knead until smooth. Chill for 20 minutes.
2 Roll out the pastry and line a 24cm/9½in loose-
bottomed tart tin. Bake 'blind' in a preheated
200°C/400°F/gas6 oven for about 15 minutes.
Remove from oven and leave to cool. Turn down
the oven to 180°C/350°F/gas4.
3 To make the filling, whisk the egg, egg yolk,
sugar and lemon zest until light and fluffy. Add the
flour and mix well, and then add the cream. Pour
into the pastry case and arrange cherries evenly.
4 Bake for about 30 minutes or until set and
golden. Allow the tart to stand for a few minutes
before lifting it out of the tin and transferring it to a
serving dish. Serve warm or cold.

Amarene al Liquore
(CHERRIES PRESERVED IN ALCOHOL)

These cherries can be eaten on their own, or with ice-cream, or in cakes, and the juice is wonderful as a digestive.

1kg/2¼lb ripe unblemished cherries
1 cinnamon stick
100g/3½oz/½cup sugar
200ml/7floz/¾cup good quality rum
bottling alcohol

1 Wash and dry the cherries and pack them tightly in a sterilized jar, adding pieces of the cinnamon stick at regular intervals.
2 Dissolve the sugar in the rum and pour onto the cherries. Fill the jar with the bottling alcohol and seal.
3 Leave the jar in a warm place, possibly in the sun, for two months, shaking and turning it every day. Then store in the pantry until needed.

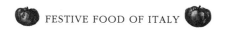

Il Palio di Siena

The word *palio* has two meanings in Italian: it is both a race and a piece of cloth, the cloth being a silk banner awarded to the winner of the race. Many such *palios*, or horse races, take place in Tuscany, the most famous of which is the world-renowned Palio di Siena, held in the town's beautiful Piazza del Campo. Two races are run, on July 2nd and August 16th, but festivities start as early as May 27th, when in the Palazzo Comunale (the town hall) the order of the horses is established by a public draw. From then on all sorts of ritual celebrations take place; the horses are blessed each in their own parish, a trial race is run, costume parades, flag-throwing competitions, and banquets and dances are organized. It is an important festival for the locals, who all contribute in some way to the success of the event, and a privileged spectacle for visitors to Siena. All who attend will eat heartily of Tuscany's rich cuisine, not least a piece of Siena's famous and morish *panforte*.

Panforte di Siena

In the 'Divine Comedy' Dante refers to Niccolo' Salimbeni, a native of Siena, who brought back from one of his trips to the Orient 'honeyed and peppered breads', and it is from this that *Panforte* is said to have developed. Traditionally a Christmas treat, it can now be bought all year round.

200g/7oz/1¼cups blanched almonds, finely chopped
115g/4oz/½cup walnut, finely chopped
115g/4oz/½cup dried figs, finely chopped
170g/6oz/¾cup candied peel, finely chopped
5ml/1teaspoon ground cinnamon
5ml/1teaspoon mixed spice
170g/6oz/½cup honey
85g/3oz/⅓cup sugar
2–4 sheets rice paper

1 In a large bowl combine the nuts, figs, peel, cinnamon and mixed spice.
2 Warm the honey in a saucepan over medium heat and as it becomes runny add the sugar and stir until dissolved. Do not let it boil. Pour over the nuts and spices and mix well.
3 Line the bottom of a 20cm/8in loose-bottomed cake tin with the rice paper and pour the mixture in; smooth out the surface and cover with the remaining rice paper, or sprinkle with flour and a little cinnamon.
4 Bake in a preheated 180°C/350°F/gas4 oven for about 30 minutes. Leave to cool in the cake ring for 10 minutes, and then take out of the tin and leave to go cold on a cooling rack.
5 Store in an airtight tin. *Panforte* is better eaten one or two days after baking. If you sprinkled it with flour, remove excess with a pastry brush before storing.

Sagra dell' Olio d'Oliva

FESTIVAL OF OLIVE OIL

The olive is the one single ingredient that distinguishes Italian cooking from any other style. Olives grow in almost all regions of Italy, and yield the best extra virgin oil in the world. Each region grows a different variety of tree and produces a different-tasting olive, from the slightly peppery taste of Tuscan olives to the sweeter, more delicate taste of Liguria oil and the almost-perfumed southern oil. The olives are harvested in November and December either by hand-picking the fallen olives or by stretching sheets under the trees and then beating or shaking the branches. Within a week of harvesting, the olives will be crushed and the oil squeezed from the pulp in special oil presses.

Oil festivals are celebrated in the late summer, to which producers bring samples of the past harvest for everyone to taste, and of course speculate on the serious matter of the new harvest. Oil is usually tasted on bread, though the experts need only rub a few drops into the warmth of the palm of their hands. While these antics go on seasonal local specialities will be on offer, with great quantities of wine, so that discussions can stretch into the evening.

28

Bruschetta

The tradition of *bruschetta* goes back to the Romans, who ate it in great quantities with *mulsum* (honeyed wine) at such festivals as the Saturnalia. The tradition of Bruschetta Festivals continues to this day in some villages. In Spello, Umbria, the *Sagra della Bruschetta* takes place at the beginning of February and the oil used at this time will still be fresh from the pressing, adding special character to this dish.

To make *bruschetta* all you need is a good round loaf of country-style Italian bread, cut in thick slices. Either grill, toast or colour it on a barbecue, and as soon as the bread starts to crisp remove from the heat, rub with a cut clove of garlic and sprinkle generously with extra virgin olive oil. Serve as an appetizer on its own or with slices of plum tomatoes and mozzarella, or instead of croûtons in a salad or as an accompaniment to a hearty soup.

Pinzimonio

(OLIVE OIL DRESSING)

Virgin olive oil is the perfect dip for fresh raw vegetables; simply season with salt and freshly ground black pepper, and add a little lemon juice or vinegar if you like. Though this is a rustic way of serving vegetables, it can make an elegant first course for a summer lunch with carefully chosen vegetables such as crispy white fennel, juicy peppers, ripe plum tomatoes, etc.

Sagra dell' Aglio

GARLIC FESTIVAL

Garlic is usually associated with the cooking of South Italy, and indeed it is widely used there in soups, with fish and vegetables, but many Northern recipes also make use of it. In the villages of Molino dei Torti, in Piedmont, and Vessolico, in Liguria, the garlic harvest is celebrated at the end of July or the beginning of August. Here, as in many other villages where garlic is grown and fêted, the crops are taken to the market square for a particularly fragrant selling and buying session. Farmers have distinctive ways of plaiting their garlic stalks and for this occasion elaborate structures of tresses, garlands and wreaths are used as white perfumed decorations to embellish the stalls. Many people take this chance to stock up with this useful ingredient. Not surprisingly, plenty of wine will be at hand to quench the thirst but also to help reduce some of the aroma left in the mouth by various tastings of garlicky *bruschettas* and *crostini* (croûtons).

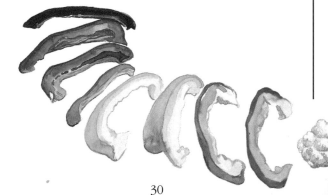

Bagna Calda
(HOT ANCHOVY SAUCE)

This is a traditional Piedmontese dish. *Bagna calda* means 'Hot sauce', and it is served in a terracotta saucepan set over a flame and kept bubbling throughout the meal. Raw and blanched vegetables are dipped in the sauce and sometimes thin strips of raw beef are added. Anchovies and garlic are the most important ingredients in this recipe; for a very creamy end result use two or three times the amount of garlic suggested below and marinate the cloves in milk overnight; add the butter and simmer until the garlic is completely soft, then proceed with the recipe.

serves 4
140g/5oz anchovy fillets
115g/4oz/½cup butter
6 garlic cloves, peeled and sliced
200ml/7fl oz/¾cup olive oil
4–5 walnuts, chopped (optional)
Fresh vegetables for dipping: fennel,
  peppers, cauliflower florets,
  roasted onions, leaves of Savoy
  cabbage, sliced and boiled
  Jerusalem artichokes, etc.

1 Gently heat the butter and garlic in an earthenware saucepan, and leave to simmer until the garlic is soft; take care not to let it burn.
2 Add the anchovies to the softened garlic and mix until dissolved.
3 Stir in the oil and walnuts and heat through.

31

Ferragosto

Ferragosto falls during August, the hottest month of the year when the Italians take their holidays, and shops and offices are closed. The name derives from *Feriae, Augustae*, a festival declared to celebrate the emperor Augustus on the first day of the month named after him. Many other Roman festivals were celebrated during August, including one in honour of a god of abundance, Ops, from whose name is derived the word 'opulence'. Nowadays the August festival of *Ferragosto* is celebrated on the 15th; the day in the Christian calendar 45AD when it is believed the Virgin Mary ascended to Heaven.

This combination of pagan and religious history is typical of many Italian festivals; though it represents for many a day of rest and fun it is mixed with reverence and respect for the Virgin Mary. As many churches are dedicated to her this day becomes a special feast day in many villages. Statues are taken in procession along the main streets before being returned to the church and blessed; and villagers can then fall to more earthly enjoyment in the shape of food and wine.

More generally, it is a day to forget about work, to eat, drink and be merry, and many people choose to escape the towns and cities to the coast, to eat in style, sampling festive and regional dishes in the many restaurants and resorts, or in the peace and quiet of the countryside with a picnic.

Bomba di Riso alla Piacentina
(RICE 'BOMBE' PIACENZA STYLE)

550g/1¼lb/2cups Arborio or pudding rice
1 large pigeon, cleaned and boned
115g/4oz/½cup butter
1 small onion, finely chopped
40ml/2tablespoons/3tablespoons dry white wine
400g/14oz tin of plum tomatoes, drained and
   chopped
3 fresh sage leaves, finely chopped
4 tablespoons/⅓cup grated Parmesan
2 eggs
4–5 tablespoons dried breadcrumbs
salt and freshly ground pepper

1 Sweat the onion in half the butter for a few
minutes, then add the pieces of boned pigeon and
leave to colour. Deglaze with the wine, add the
tomatoes and sage, and season. Simmer for about
10 minutes, remove and keep warm.
2 Cook the rice in boiling salted water until 'al
dente', drain, rinse with cold water and drain
again.
3 Stir into the rice the sauce, the remaining butter
(save a few pieces for dotting the top), the
Parmesan and the eggs.
4 Grease an ovenproof dish, preferably a bowl,
and line with two-thirds of the breadcrumbs.
Arrange two-thirds of the rice mixture in the bowl.
Make a well in the centre; into this put the pigeon,
cover with the remaining rice, sprinkle with
breadcrumbs and dot with a few pieces of butter.
5 Bake in a preheated 180°C/350°F/gas4 oven for
about 45 minutes or until golden and crunchy on
top. Remove from the oven, leave to stand for
about 10 minutes and then turn out onto a serving
plate.

Arista allia Fiorentina
(ROAST LOIN OF PORK FLORENCE STYLE)

Some date the origin of this dish to 1430 when a group of Greek bishops attended an ecumenical council in Florence called by Pope Eugenius IV. Roast loin of pork was served at one of the banquets and was quickly dubbed *aristos* (the best) by one of the bishops... and the name stuck. Others say it comes from the Latin *arista* (top part), in this case the saddle.

This roast is often cooked on a spit but when roasting in the oven use the fat released during cooking to roast potatoes to be served with the meat.

serves 6
1.5kg/3½lb loin of pork, boned, rolled and tied
2 garlic cloves
3–4 sprigs of rosemary
salt and freshly ground pepper

1 Chop the garlic and rosemary together. Make small incisions in the fat of the roast and rub in the garlic and rosemary. Season well.
2 Roast in a preheated 190°C/375°F/gas5 oven for about 1½ hours, basting and turning the meat occasionally.

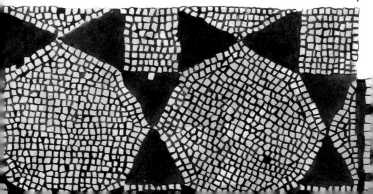

Gelo di Melone
(WATERMELON JELLY)

This is a traditional dish made in Palermo in Sicily for *Ferragosto*; a lemon and a jasmine version are also made for this occasion.

serves 6–8
1 ripe watermelon, weighing about 5kg/11lb
700g/1⅔lb/3cups sugar
250g/8½oz/2¼cups arrowroot or potato starch
5ml/1teaspoon vanilla essence
100g/3½oz/½cup bitter chocolate, chopped
100g/3½oz/½cup candied fruit, chopped
30g/1oz/¼cup pistachios, peeled and finely
   chopped
ground cinnamon

1 Remove the pulp from the watermelon and pass it through a sieve. Add the sugar and arrowroot or starch.
2 Gently heat the melon mix, and then simmer for a few minutes. Remove from heat and stir in the vanilla essence. Leave to cool.
3 When almost cold mix in the chocolate, candied fruit and pistachios. Pour into wet individual moulds or into one large mould and leave to set in the refrigerator for at least 2–3 hours (preferably overnight).
4 Turn onto serving plates and sprinkle with cinnamon.

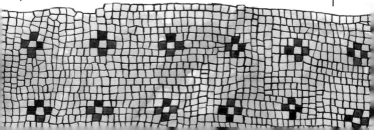

Sagra delle Cozze e Pesce

FESTIVAL OF MUSSELS AND FISH

The Mediterranean shores of Italy offer a wide variety of fish and shellfish, and coastal towns and villages boast spectacular fish markets. One such fishing centre is Taranto, which celebrates during September a feast in honour of 'Stella Maris' (the Star of the Sea), who is said to protect the fishermen when out in their boats. Blessed with ideal conditions to raise shellfish, Taranto has been famous since its first Spartan settlers in 706BC for its clams, mussels, sea urchins, oysters (including the ones used to produce the purple dye of Roman emperors' togas), and Taranto is still the principal supplier to the rest of Italy. Because of the high quality of the fish, locals tend to eat raw fish fresh from the sea, bought from the long line of fish stalls along the seafront selling the catch of the day. But during the festivities special barbecue fires are lit on the seafront and fish is grilled or fried and consumed in the open as the boats return; large quantities of mussels, clams and oysters are offered, so that everyone has a chance to enjoy what is considered the pride of the town.

Cozze Ripiene al Sugo
(STUFFED MUSSELS IN TOMATO SAUCE)

serves 4

1kg/2¼lb large mussels, washed and scrubbed
75ml/5tablespoons/⅓cup olive oil
2 garlic cloves
400g/14oz tin of plum tomatoes, chopped
sprig of basil, chopped
bunch of flat-leafed parsley, chopped
2 eggs
3–4 tablespoons dried breadcrumbs
salt and freshly ground pepper

1 With a sharp knife open each mussel without separating the two valves. Wash well in salted water and drain.
2 To make the sauce, heat the oil in a saucepan and add one garlic clove; leave to flavour the oil and remove as it starts to colour. Add the tomatoes, a little water (the sauce should be sufficient to cover the mussels), and the basil. Season and simmer for 15–20 minutes.
3 For the stuffing, mix together the parsley, eggs, the remaining garlic clove, finely chopped, and enough breadcrumbs to make a moist mixture.
4 Stuff each mussel with the mixture, close the two valves and tie with sewing thread. Add the mussels to the tomato sauce and simmer for 15–20 minutes.
5 Untie the mussels and serve hot with rice or pasta.

Frittura di Cozze
(DEEP-FRIED MUSSELS)

Serve these mussels as a starter or as appetizers with drinks.

serves 4
1kg/2¼lb mussels, washed and scrubbed
225g/8oz/2cups plain flour
2 eggs, beaten
250g/8½oz/2½cups dried breadcrumbs
olive oil for deep-frying
salt
lemon wedges to serve

1 With a sharp knife remove and discard one half of the mussel shell, taking care not to damage the molluscs. Wash the half shells with the mussels in slightly salted water, drain well and pat dry.
2 Toss in the flour, then dip in beaten egg and finally in breadcrumbs.
3 Fry a few mussels at a time in hot oil until golden. Pile on a serving plate, sprinkle with salt and serve with lemon wedges.

Calamari Sott'Aceto
(SQUID PRESERVED IN VINEGAR)

In Puglia this dish is prepared with octopus. It will be good to eat after only a few days, as an appetizer or as part of a seafood salad.

900g/2lb baby squids, cleaned, gutted and washed
bunch of fresh mint
4–5 garlic cloves, peeled and sliced
white wine vinegar

1 Bring a large pot of water to the boil and blanch the baby squid for a few minutes until tender. (If using large squid, skin them and cut them into rounds; they may also need longer cooking.)
2 Drain well and pack into jars, alternating the squid with layers of fresh mint leaves and slices of garlic. Fill the jar with vinegar and seal.

Pesci Fritti All'Agliata
(MARINATED FRIED FISH)

Variations of this recipe can be found throughout Italy, from vinegar and sage to minted tomato sauce with garlic or a simple mixture of herbs. It can be eaten as a starter or a main course.

serves 4
900g/2lb whole, small fish such as sardines, sole, trout, etc., gutted and washed
225g/8oz/2cups plain flour
olive oil for frying
sprig each of rosemary, sage and oregano
2 garlic cloves, chopped
white wine vinegar
salt

1 Toss the fish in seasoned flour and shallow fry in the oil until golden. Arrange in a deep serving dish.
2 Heat 2–3 tablespoons of fresh oil in a pan, and fry the herbs and garlic for a few seconds. Add the vinegar, heat through and pour over fish.
3 Leave to marinate for a few hours or overnight, and serve cold.

Sagra delle Lenticchie

LENTIL FESTIVAL

The best lentils produced in Italy come from Abruzzi, a region rich in culinary traditions. The countryside surrounding the village of S. Stefano di Sassano is known for its excellent crop of small, dark lentils, which maintain their shape during the short time needed to cook them and are said to be some of the tastiest in the world. The village celebrates its crop every year during the harvest in late September, when the short flat pods are collected from the bushy lentil plants and gathered in crates and sacks. As the picking is still done by hand the end of the harvest means party time for all those involved. When all the work is finished, growers, villagers and pickers gather together in the main square where the festivities start; and of course lentils find their way onto the menu in the form of a hearty lentil stew eaten with locally produced sausages, pork ribs and plenty of local wine.

Zuppa di Lenticchie Abruzzese

(LENTIL SOUP ABRUZZI-STYLE)

serves 4

200g/7oz brown lentils, soaked overnight and drained

2 bay leaves

100ml/4fl oz/½cup olive oil

20 roasted chestnuts, peeled and chopped

115g/4oz streaky bacon, diced (optional)

sprig of thyme

sprig of marjoram

400g/14oz tin of plum tomatoes, chopped
4 large slices of country-style bread, thinly cut
salt and freshly ground pepper

1 Simmer the lentils with the bay leaves in boiling water until tender.
2 Meanwhile heat half the oil in a saucepan, add the chestnuts and bacon if using and fry for a few minutes. Add the thyme and marjoram and then the tomatoes. Season and simmer for 5–10 minutes.
3 Combine the lentils and cooking liquid with the tomato sauce and simmer for a further 10 minutes.
4 Fry the bread slices in the remaining olive oil or grill them and brush them with the oil. Place one slice of bread in each serving bowl and ladle soup over it. Serve immediately with freshly ground black pepper.

Lenticchie in Umido
(STEWED LENTILS)

serves 4
285g/10oz brown lentils soaked overnight and drained
85g/3oz Pancetta (Italian bacon), diced
1 small onion, chopped
5 sage leaves, chopped
salt and freshly ground pepper

1 Gently heat the Pancetta in a saucepan until it starts releasing its fat, then add the onion and sage and fry for a few minutes.
2 Add the lentils and cover with water. Simmer gently for about 1 hour until all the water is absorbed and the lentils are tender. Season and serve.

Sagra del Sedano D'Oro

FESTIVAL OF THE GOLDEN CELERY

The ancient Romans wore celery wreaths in the belief that celery was a cure for hangovers; they also decorated family tombs with it, and ate it as a dessert, cooked with honey and pepper. Celery is said to be good for the health, and some people claim it has aphrodisiac qualities if eaten raw in large enough quantity. It is certainly eaten and enjoyed all over Italy, where many varieties are grown. In Central and Southern Italy the fat, juicy stalks are eaten raw, dipped in *pinzimonio* (olive oil dressing), or tomato sauce, or as part of a salad; in Liguria it is often eaten with olives, Pecorino and crusty bread as an appetizer, and in Friuli a traditional celery soup is served on Christmas Eve.

The best celery is produced in Tuscany and Umbria, and at the end of September the village of Figlini Valdarno celebrates the festival of the *Sedano d'Oro* . All the market stalls make way for baskets of golden celery and each farmer enters his best specimens in the contest for the perfect head of celery.

Sedani alla Pratese
(TUSCAN-STYLE STUFFED CELERY)

serves 6
2 large, tender heads of celery
50ml/3tablespoons/¼cup olive oil
1 medium onion, chopped
200g/7oz chicken livers, cleaned and chopped
115g/4oz each Parma and cooked ham, finely
    diced
115g/4oz minced veal
200g/7oz mushrooms (preferably wild), chopped
150ml/¼pint/⅔cup dry white wine
225g/8oz/2cups plain flour
150ml/¼pint/⅔cup milk
pinch of grated nutmeg
3 tablespoons/¼cup grated Parmesan
2 eggs, beaten
250g/8½oz/2½cups dried breadcrumbs
olive oil for frying
salt and freshly ground pepper

1 Strip off the celery stalks, cut them into 7cm/3in
pieces and blanch in boiling, lightly salted water.
When just tender, refresh in cold water and drain.
2 Heat the olive oil in a saucepan, add the onions
and when coloured add the liver, hams, veal and
mushrooms. Simmer for a few minutes and then
add the white wine.
3 When the wine has almost totally evaporated
sprinkle in 1 tablespoon of the flour and stir in the
milk, nutmeg and Parmesan. Season and cook,
stirring continuously until the mixture has
thickened enough to stuff the celery stalks.
4 Remove from heat and stuff each piece of celery
with a little mixture then toss in the flour, dip in
the egg and finally cover with breadcrumbs.
5 Shallow-fry a few pieces at a time until golden.
Serve hot.

Sagra dei Funghi e dei Tartufi

FESTIVAL OF WILD MUSHROOMS AND TRUFFLES

During the mushroom season from the end of September to November, Italians all over the country begin the serious ritual of mushroom hunting. Rising early in the morning, not only at weekends but sometimes before going to work, they venture into the woods kitted with woven baskets (any other kind of carrier could damage the spoils of the search), walking sticks, short knives and Wellington boots, and the hope of a good catch. Everyone has a favourite place to go and this closely guarded secret is not shared with just anyone but passed from generation to generation (I was shown by my father where my grandparents hunted for ceps and chanterelles). Finding even just one mushroom is an elating experience and there is a magical feeling while hunting, probably because one is walking through the woods in the silence and stillness of the early autumn mist.

During the month of October, towns and villages hold festivals where many varieties of mushrooms are put on show in baskets lined with chestnut or fern leaves. All the edible varieties will be on sale, and the bartering and bargaining is mingled with boastful stories from the more seasoned hunters.

Even the most overfilled basket, however, will be overshadowed by the find of one small truffle. White truffles are particularly sought after and are found only in Italy, particularly around Alba, in Piedmont. The festival the town organizes to

celebrate the white truffle is attended by
international chefs and gourmets and by buyers
from all over the world, as well as the locals.
Auctions are held for large quantities but individual
truffles can be bought from the hunters; and of
course wine and other local delicacies are at hand
to help along the festivities.

Mushrooms need to be consumed almost
immediately and well dried; when possible simply
brush off earth deposits or use a damp cloth. Small,
firm ceps can be preserved in oil after having been
blanched in vinegared water, and served during the
winter as an appetizer. Some species can be frozen
and then added to soups and stews. Ceps are
probably the most versatile and, like morels, can
be bought dried all the year round.

Polenta coi Funghi
(POLENTA WITH WILD MUSHROOM RAGOUT)

serves 4

Polenta
1½litres/2½pints/6¼cups milk
300g/10½oz/2cups maize flour
115g/4oz/½cup butter
salt and freshly ground pepper

Mushroom ragout
550g/1¼lb mixed wild mushrooms, cleaned and
    roughly cut
70ml/4tablespoons/⅓cup olive oil
1 medium onion, finely chopped
3 garlic cloves, finely chopped
50ml/3tablespoons/¼cup dry white wine
115g/4oz/½cup butter
juice of ½ lemon
40ml/2tablespoons/3tablespoons flat-leafed parsley,
    finely chopped
salt and freshly ground pepper

1 To make the *polenta,* heat the milk and season
well. When it starts to simmer gradually whisk in
the maize flour. Simmer for about 45 minutes,
stirring from time to time. Add the butter and mix.
2 To make the *ragout*, heat the oil in a saucepan,
add the onion and garlic, and leave to colour. Add
the mushrooms and fry for a few minutes, then add
the white wine and a couple of tablespoons of
water. Cover and simmer for about 15 minutes.
3 Remove the lid and allow most of the juices to
evaporate, then incorporate the butter and lemon
juice. Stir in the parsley, check seasoning and serve
immediately with the *polenta.*

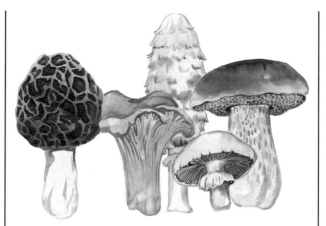

Funghi al Fungitiello
(WILD MUSHROOM STEW)

Serve with *bruschetta* or *polenta* or with roast quails.

serves 4
1kg/2¼lb mixed wild mushrooms, cleaned and
    roughly cut
75ml/5tablespoons/⅓cup olive oil
2 garlic cloves, crushed
400g/14oz tin plum tomatoes, chopped
2–3 tablespoons flat-leafed parsley, chopped
1 small chilli, seeded and finely chopped
salt

1 Heat the oil with the garlic; when it starts to
sizzle add the mushrooms and fry for a few
minutes.
2 Add the tomatoes and leave to simmer for
10–15 minutes until the stew has thickened a little.
3 Add the parsley and chilli, check seasoning and
serve.

Crostini ai Tartufi
(TRUFFLE CROÛTONS)

100g/3½oz truffles, preferably white, finely sliced
20ml/1tablespoon/1½tablespoons olive oil
115g/4oz/½cup butter
1 anchovy fillet
⅓ small garlic clove, finely chopped
5ml/1 teaspoon flat-leafed parsley, finely chopped
4 slices of good white bread, crust removed and
    cut into small squares or triangles

1 Heat the oil and a third of the butter in a
saucepan, add the anchovy, garlic and parsley and
leave to simmer for a couple of minutes.
2 Add the truffle slices and leave to infuse over
low heat for about 5 minutes.
3 Meanwhile, fry the croûtons in the remaining
butter.
4 Spread a little truffle sauce on each croûton and
enjoy.

Risotto ai Tartufi
(TRUFFLE RISOTTO)

serves 4

350g/12oz/1¼cups arborio rice
140g/5oz/¾cup butter
1 small onion, finely chopped
100ml/4fl oz/½cup dry white wine
1litre/1¾pints/4½cups meat or chicken stock
115g/4oz/1cup grated Parmesan
1 small white truffle

1 Melt half the butter in a saucepan, add the onion and leave to colour. Add the rice and fry for a couple of minutes.
2 Add the white wine to the rice and simmer to evaporate. Heat the stock separately until simmering and add to the rice, a few ladles at a time, stirring continuously and allowing the stock to be absorbed between additions. The rice should take about 20 minutes to cook and have a creamy texture but each grain should still have 'bite'.
3 Check seasoning, and add the remaining butter and the Parmesan. Cover and leave to stand for a few minutes. Serve sprinkled with truffle shavings.

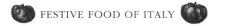

Sagra delle Castagne

CHESTNUT FESTIVAL

The autumn heralds for children in Italy the beginning of the 'conker' season, and for everyone else the pleasure of roasting and eating chestnuts over open fires in special iron pans with perforated bottoms to allow the flames to scorch the shiny brown skins and make peeling the chestnuts easier.

Many types of chestnut contain three or four nuts in each shell but the best type are those that yield just one or two nuts. Piedmont, Lombardy and Veneto have a great number of chestnut trees, many growing wild, and in these regions villages celebrate the harvest with great bonfires, in which the nuts are roasted. Popular in these regions are autumn chestnut soups, tarts and rich cakes, made with chestnut flour, and from the crops gathered near Aosta a most delicious but extremely rich chestnut cream is made, often used to make Mont Blanc, a concoction of sweet chestnut purée, whipped cream and grated chocolate.

Minestra di Riso, Latte e Castagne
(RICE, MILK AND CHESTNUT SOUP)

You can use dried chestnuts for this but soak for at least one day before cooking.

serves 4
200g/7oz fresh chestnuts, skinned
2 litres/3½pints/9cups water
140g/5oz/¾cup risotto or pudding rice
500ml/16fl oz/2cups milk
30g/1oz butter
salt and a pinch of ground cinnamon

1 Put chestnuts in a large saucepan and cover with the water. Salt and bring to the boil. Simmer for around 1½ hours.
2 Add the rice and when the rice is half-cooked incorporate the milk and butter. Simmer until the soup has reached a creamy consistency. Serve hot sprinkled with a little cinnamon.

Castagne Bergamasche
(CHESTNUTS BERGAMO-STYLE)
serves 4–6
1kg/2¼lb hot roasted chestnuts
70ml/4tablespoons/⅓cup Grappa (eau de vie)
2–3tablespoons sugar

1 Quickly peel the chestnuts while still hot. Toss them dry in a frying pan (do not use any butter or oil) over a high heat.
2 Remove from heat and sprinkle with the Grappa and the sugar. Quickly mix and flambé (the heated spirit will light with a match). Eat as soon as the flames disappear.

Festa dei Morti

ALL SOULS' DAY

The tradition of remembering the dead dates from prehistoric times, and all cultures have some form of ritual to express respect and veneration towards deceased loved ones. In the Christian calendar the first two days of November are set aside for the commemoration of the dead. November 1st is All Saints' Day, a Holy day of Obligation when all the saints who are not celebrated on any particular day during the year are remembered and prayed to. November 2nd is All Souls' Day, commemorating all the faithful departed, and on this day of mourning and rejoicing families visit the graves of their loved ones, bringing flowers and wreaths. Italians maintain strong family ties, and this celebration is a deeply felt one.

At one time offerings of food would be left on the graves, and from this derives the tradition of leaving small breads, sweets, beans and lentils on the kitchen table at night with the windows ajar to allow the dead to enter, see the offerings and hear the prayers said in their honour. This custom is still practised in some southern villages.

Special cakes are eaten at this time, and biscuits made in the form of broad beans, *Fave dei Morti*, an association dating back to Egyptian times, when it was believed that the beans contained souls of loved ones.

Pan di Mort
(BREAD FOR THE DEAD)

Serve these biscuits with coffee, or a sweet white wine.

makes 20–25
450g/1lb Amaretti biscuits, ground
285g/10oz/1¼cups sugar
225g/8oz/2cups plain flour
115g/4oz/1cup ground almonds
5ml/1teaspoon baking powder
5ml/1teaspoon ground cinnamon
115g/4oz/½cup sultanas, soaked in warm water
115g/4oz/½cup dried figs, chopped
4 egg whites
70ml/4tablespoons/⅓cup dry white wine
4–5 sheets of rice paper
icing sugar for sprinkling

1 Mix together all dry ingredients and the drained sultanas and figs.

2 Make a well in the centre and add the egg whites and enough white wine to form a dough. Knead vigorously for about 10 minutes.

3 Shape the dough into small, flat elongated breads and place each on a piece of rice paper.

4 Bake in a preheated 180°C/350°F/gas4 oven for about 20–25 minutes, until the breads are dry all the way through. Cool, sprinkle with icing sugar and serve. They can be eaten immediately or stored for a few days in an airtight container.

Vigilia di Natale

CHRISTMAS EVE

Christmas Eve in Italy is spent, as in many other countries, with the family, adding the last few touches to the Christmas tree – coloured lights, glass balls, streamers, mandarin oranges and sweets or pieces of *torrone* (nougat) in decorative boxes. In preparation for the feasting of Christmas Day, and as a sign of respect for the Body of Christ, Christmas Eve is a *giorno di magro* (a lean day) and no meat is consumed. In most households fish will be served for lunch and dinner, and in Central and Southern Italy this is likely to be eel, either as a main course or as part of a rice or pasta dish.

Fettucini con la Mollica

(FETTUCINI WITH DRIED BREADCRUMBS)

serves 4

Pasta
200g/7oz/1¾cups plain flour
pinch of salt
2 eggs
140g/5oz/1¼cups semolina

Sauce
100ml/4fl oz/½cup olive oil
1 small garlic clove
5 anchovy fillets
½ small chilli, seeded and chopped (optional)
90g/3¼oz/1cup dried breadcrumbs
salt and freshly ground pepper

1 First make the pasta. Sift the flour and salt onto a clean, dry working surface, make a well in the centre and break into it the eggs. Gently mix to form a dough and knead for about 10–15 minutes until the dough is smooth and fairly dry. Cover and leave to rest in a cool place for about 15 minutes.

2 Divide the dough into 6 pieces and roll out thinly, using either a rolling pin or a pasta machine. Leave the pasta sheets to dry for a few minutes.

3 Cut into thin strips by rolling up each sheet and with a sharp knife cutting across the roll. Unroll the strips and toss in the semolina (the semolina absorbs excess moisture and speeds up the drying of the pasta).

4 Cook the pasta in boiling salted water for 3–4 minutes, taking care not to overdo it.

5 While the pasta is cooking, heat half the oil in a saucepan with the garlic clove; as soon as it starts to colour remove it, add the anchovies and cook gently to allow the anchovies to dissolve. Add the chilli if using.

6 Drain the pasta and dress with the remaining olive oil and the anchovy sauce. Toss well, season, sprinkle with breadcrumbs and serve immediately.

Natale

CHRISTMAS

Christmas is very much a family feast in Italy. As in countries the world over, the early morning is a time for the children, for the race to the tree or the *presepio* (the crib) to see and open the presents. Savouring a glass of good *prosecco* (an Italian dry sparkling wine) or uncorking a vintage bottle are left to the older generations, and the ritual of preparing the festive table and the celebratory meal is a joint effort enjoyed by all.

Friends and relatives drop in to exchange presents and good wishes, and sweet 'niblets' are prepared to welcome them: nougat, nuts, spicy biscuits and, my favourite, plump figs stuffed with nuts and peel and then dipped in chocolate, a speciality of southern Italy.

There is no fixed standard Christmas meal, as each region serves its best produce; the greatest regional influence will be reflected in the *antipasti* (appetizers), which will include anything from Parma ham, *Bresaola* (cured fillet of beef), preserved mushrooms, olives and pickled vegetables and fish. Stuffed pasta is usually served as a first course, either in the shape of *ravioli* or *tortellini*, which are said to have been offered as Christmas gifts to priests and monks during the twelfth century. A roast will follow, most often some kind of bird, turkey in Lombardy and capon in Central Italy, but always accompanied by potatoes, vegetables and salads. The traditional end to the meal is now almost always *Panettone*, served warm with a glass of sparkling wine or stuffed with ice-cream, Mascarpone or Ricotta, and some regions also serve traditional home-made cakes rich in candied fruits, sultanas and raisins.

Agnolotti
(PIEDMONTESE RAVIOLI)

Agnolotti are often poached in meat stock and served like a soup; they can also be dressed with the sauce from a roast or with a light tomato sauce.

serves 6–8
Pasta
550g/1¼lb/4cups plain flour
3 eggs
175ml/6fl oz/¾cup water

Filling
400g/14oz cooked roast beef, finely minced
285g/10oz Italian sausages, cooked
  and minced
1kg/2¼lb spinach, blanched and chopped
pinch of nutmeg
4–5 tablespoons of grated Parmesan
3–4 eggs, beaten
salt and freshly ground pepper

225g/8oz/1cup butter
5 sage leaves, chopped

1 Make the pasta dough following the instructions for fettucine, on page 55. Cover the dough and leave in a cool place while preparing the stuffing.
2 In a bowl mix together the minced beef, sausages, spinach, nutmeg, Parmesan and enough egg to hold the stuffing together. Season.
3 Roll out one piece of dough at a time into a thin sheet and place little balls of stuffing at 5cm/2in intervals on the pasta. Roll out another sheet of dough and place on top of stuffing, pressing the two sheets together. If the dough is too dry to seal well, brush the under sheet with egg wash. Cut into squares with a pastry cutter. Place the *agnolotti* on kitchen cloths dusted with flour and continue until all the dough and filling is used up.

4 Bring a large pot of salted water to the boil, lower the heat and cook the *agnolotti* in simmering water for about 8 minutes. Drain well.

5 Heat the butter and sage in a frying pan until it starts to colour, pour over the pasta and serve immediately, sprinkled with a little extra Parmesan.

Cappone Ripieno
(STUFFED CAPON)

serves 4
1 capon, weighing about 1.1kg/2½lb
285g/10oz each veal and lean beef, minced
115g/4oz cooked ham, finely diced
115g/4oz Parma ham, finely diced
115g/4oz Mortadella (Italian salami), finely diced
100ml/4fl oz/½cup Marsala
4 egg whites
4 hardboiled egg yolks
50ml/3tablespoons/¼cup olive oil
115g/4oz/½cup butter
salt and freshly ground pepper

1 Taking care not to rip the skin, remove the breast from the boned capon, cut into thin strips and set aside.

2 Mix together the veal, beef, hams and Mortadella, add the Marsala and egg whites, season and mix well.

3 Stuff the capon with the mixture, placing at regular intervals strips of the breast and quarters of the hardboiled yolks. Reshape the bird and sew the back with thread or tie neatly.

4 Place on a roasting tray, sprinkle with the oil and dot with the butter, and roast in a preheated 180°C/350°F/gas4 oven for about 1½ hours. Leave to stand for at least 15 minutes before carving.

Panettone

The name of this cake is said to come from a
Milanese baker Antonio (Toni), who concocted it
to impress a girlfriend around Christmas time in the
fifteenth century; the result was so successful not
just with the girl but with many of his other clients
that 'Pan de Toni' became a regular feature in the
Christmas season.

25g/1oz fresh yeast
150ml/¼pint/⅔cup lukewarm milk
400g/14oz/3½cups plain flour
1 egg
2 egg yolks
45g/1½oz/⅙cup sugar
5ml/1teaspoon vanilla essence
170g/6oz/¾cup butter, melted
85g/3oz/⅓cup candied fruit, chopped
85g/3oz/⅓cup sultanas
zest of 1 orange, finely grated

1 Cream the yeast in a small bowl with 2
tablespoons of the warm milk. Add 2 tablespoons
of the flour and a pinch of sugar, mix to a batter,
cover and leave to foam in a warm place
(approximately 30 minutes).
2 Beat the egg and egg yolks with the sugar,
vanilla essence and two-thirds of the melted butter.
3 Sift the flour into a warm bowl, and mix
together the yeast mixture and egg mixture. Make a
well in the centre of the flour and pour in the yeast
and egg mixture, and then the remaining warm
milk. Knead until you have a smooth, shiny dough.
Grease a clean bowl, place the dough in it, cover
and leave to prove in a warm place for about 1–2
hours, until doubled in size.

4 Turn the dough onto a lightly floured surface and knead for about 5 minutes more. Leave to prove again until doubled in volume.

5 Meanwhile, prepare a 15cm/6in tin at least 7.5cm/3in deep; tie a foil collar around it to double its depth (the tin should now be 15cm/6in deep). Gently grease the tin and foil, and line the bottom of the tin with greased greaseproof paper.

6 Knock back the dough after the second proving and incorporate the candied fruit, sultanas and zest.

7 Shape into a ball, place in the prepared tin and with a sharp knife score the top. Bake in a preheated 200°C/400°F/gas6 oven for 10 minutes, then brush with the remaining melted butter, lower the heat to 180°C/350°F/gas4 and bake for a further 45 minutes or until a skewer inserted in the middle comes out dry.

8 Leave the *panettone* to stand for 5 minutes before removing the collar and lifting out of the tin. Serve cold.